The Vimy Oaks

A Journey to Peace

Linda Granfield

illustrated by
Brian Deines

North Winds Press
An Imprint of Scholastic Canada Ltd.

In memory of my cousin, Thomas Ivan Proudler (1899–1917).
Still a boy when he fought and died on Vimy Ridge.
Still over there.
— L.G.

For Jack, Jeff and Mike.
— B.D.

The paintings in this book are created in oil on canvas.

*All italicized quotations in the book are from various pages
in Leslie H. Miller's war diaries.*

Library and Archives Canada Cataloguing in Publication
Granfield, Linda, author
The Vimy oaks : a journey to peace / Linda Granfield ;
illustrated by Brian Deines.

ISBN 978-1-4431-4850-4 (hardback)

1. Miller, Leslie H., 1889-1979--Juvenile literature. 2. Vimy
Memorial (France)--Juvenile literature. 3. War memorials--France--
Juvenile literature. 4. War memorials--Ontario--Juvenile literature.
5. World War, 1914-1918--Monuments--France--Juvenile literature.
6. World War, 1914-1918--Monuments--Ontario--Juvenile literature.
7. Vimy Ridge, Battle of, France, 1917--Juvenile literature. 8. Tree
planting--Juvenile literature. 9. Memorialization--Juvenile literature.
10. Soldiers--Canada--Biography--Juvenile literature. I. Deines, Brian,
illustrator II. Title.

D663.G73 2017   j940.4'65   C2016-904609-5

www.scholastic.ca

6 5 4 3 2 1   Printed in Canada 114   17 18 19 20 21

MIX
Paper from
responsible sources
FSC® C016245

"Our march [in France] led up the side of a valley, the slope heavily wooded with grand old elms, beeches, chestnuts . . . The trees were all in rows skirting the road, or in groves, evidently planted there many years ago. To see the beauty of these splendid groves both from the inside and as a part of the general landscape was sufficient evidence to convince anyone of the wisdom of planting trees."

Leslie H. Miller, October 1915

On a hot summer day in 1951, Monty McDonald and his family were out for a drive. As they bumped along Kennedy Road, a narrow dirt-and-gravel route in the countryside east of Toronto, they saw a sign near a driveway.

"The VYE-mee Oaks," Monty said slowly, as he read the top line out loud. "What's that?" he asked his father.

"It's pronounced VIM-ee," replied Sandy McDonald. "Vimy is a place in France where there was an important battle in a war. Let's go and see why it's the name of this farm."

And Sandy slowly turned the McDonald car into the driveway. Into history.

Farmer Leslie Howard Miller greeted the McDonalds that day. He showed them around the property that had been in his family for a long time, and where he had been born in 1889. The vegetable fields were ripening; fruit was heavy on the boughs.

And there were many kinds of trees, not just fruit trees. Fragrant cedar and rows of prickly spruce. Sugar maple, white birch and pine. The towering black walnut trees that edged a section of the farm were part of the Miller family

history. Like other early settlers in Ontario, Leslie Miller's ancestors knew that thriving black walnut trees were a sign that the pioneers would have good soil to farm, wood for their cabins and fences, and nuts to eat.

When the McDonalds met the Millers that summer day, shady oak trees stood in a row nearby like soldiers at attention. Just as others like them had once stood along Vimy Ridge, across the sea in France. Before the Great War changed everything.

Don't be Alarmed, the Canadians are on guard..

When the First World War, also called the Great War, began in August 1914, no one knew that millions of young men and women would die before the conflict ended in 1918. No one knew that villages would be completely destroyed, or that entire nations would be changed forever. In fact, people thought the war would be over before Christmas.

There was no single reason why the war began. Some countries wanted more power, or feared other nations' growing fleets and industrial strength. Others wanted revenge for past wrongs. So when the heir to the Austro-Hungarian throne was murdered, in June 1914, people were primed for war.

Patriotic postcards and posters beckoned young Canadian men to join the army. They also assured families that they could feel protected at home.

In 1915, a long line of streetcars on Portage Avenue, Winnipeg, Manitoba, pauses as new recruits march off to war. Women, men too old and boys too young to fight watch the troops leave the city.

When the German army moved into neutral Belgium, Britain upheld its treaty obligations to defend the Belgians. On August 4, 1914, the British government announced: "War, Germany, act." Britain, joined by other supportive countries called "Allies," was at war.

When Canada joined the war, Leslie Miller was teaching school in Saskatchewan. By the end of 1914, Leslie travelled to Winnipeg, Manitoba, to enlist in the Canadian Expeditionary Force. He was twenty-five years old and well educated; he knew Latin, Greek and Hebrew and he could speak French and German fluently. Older than many of the teenaged soldiers, and previously trained in other military groups, Leslie had lots to offer to the army's Signal Corps. In February 1915, he and other troops sailed to England.

During the winter of 1914–15, Leslie posed in uniform for this portrait taken in Winnipeg. He later told his brother Carman that the Winnipeg weather "was severe, with a lot of snow."

1915

Folkstone, England,

Leslie had this portrait taken while stationed at Shorncliffe Camp, a military base near Folkestone, England. During the First World War, millions of troops sailed across the English Channel to France from Folkestone, or returned there from France when injured or on leave.

A white flag with a blue stripe was used to signal against dark backgrounds. A solid blue flag was better seen against the day sky or light backgrounds.

Leslie, standing on the far left, poses with a Canadian Signal Corps group. He holds the blue and white flags used to send messages.

Members of the Canadian Signal Corps had important and dangerous jobs. During wartime, armies send and receive messages about troop locations and times for attacks, and warnings about the enemy. And the enemy must not intercept those messages. Signallers had to install telephone wires and cables in the muddy trenches, send information in Morse code across long distances and translate messages into other languages, often while situated very near the fighting. Many signallers were killed performing their duties.

Some Signal Corps members used bicycles or motorcycles to carry messages; some just ran quickly. Trained pigeons carried tiny paper messages attached to their legs. There was plenty of equipment to operate, carry, keep clear of mud and repair. Leslie's teaching experience meant that he was first stationed in England to train other signallers. Six months later, Leslie sailed across the English Channel to the deadly battlefields of northeast France and Belgium.

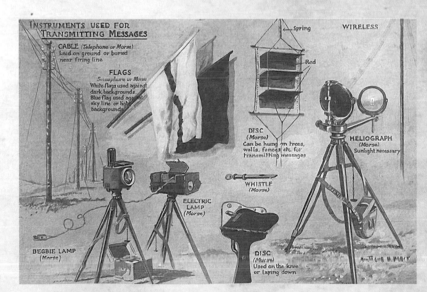

Mirrors were an important part of some transmitting instruments a signaller used. The heliograph (right) used sunlight, a mirror and shutters moved by the signaller to send messages via Morse code.

To keep the enemy from intercepting their mail and learning about troop plans, soldiers could never write in their letters about exactly where they were located. But many soldiers kept diaries of their time away at war. Writing in the small books helped them focus on something other than the long waits for food, for a bath, for more training, for mail from home, for engaging in battle.

Leslie filled the pages of his diary with observations about the people he met and the landscape around him, and bits about his job as a member of the Signal Corps. He listed books he enjoyed and concerts or silent films he saw while on leave in England. After a few days away, Leslie would be back in France, translating or sending messages in the dangerous trenches during battles, or suffering from trench fever.

Leslie sketched in his diary if he saw an interesting way of growing saplings. He identified trees and wildflowers he saw. Those small bits of living, vibrant colour he found in the devastation along the army's marches brought him comfort — and ideas for the Miller farm back in Canada.

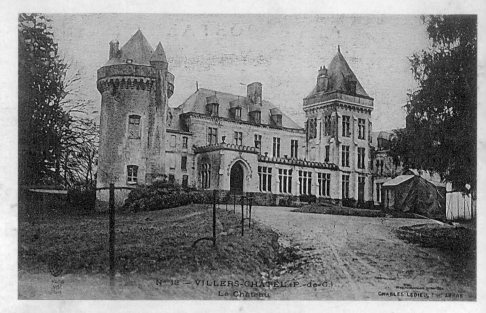

N° 18 — VILLERS-CHÂTEL (P.-de-C.)
Le Château

Leslie liked to hike when lulls in the battles allowed him the opportunity. On the grounds of the fourteenth-century château in the town of Villers-Châtel, he made note of the splendid beech trees.

"We are in a dugout some six or eight feet below ground with a covered passage leading in. It is so dark that we have to burn candles both day and night . . . the trench bottoms are covered with water, the sides are greasy and falling in places."

Leslie H. Miller

Soldiers' diaries usually fit into their pockets. One of Leslie's diaries was 11 by 19 cm (4 by 7 in.) and was filled with his tidy handwriting and sketches of what he observed. Here is his sketch of the arching beeches he saw at the château.

"The château woods are remarkable for the great number of fine old trees of many kinds. . . . The grounds from front to rear [are] lined on each side . . . with magnificent beeches . . . with 50 ft bare trunk[s] and interlaced branches above."
Leslie H. Miller

As the war continued for years, the lands of many countries endured continuous bombardment. Beautiful forests became splintered ruins in muddy fields. Villages were abandoned.

In April 1917, Leslie and his fellow signallers were still dodging danger while taking and sending messages along the 14-kilometre-long Vimy Ridge in France. At dawn on a snowy Monday, April 9, in a carefully planned and executed attack, thousands of Canadian soldiers fought the German army on the ridge. It took four days and nights of hand-to-hand fighting and bombardments, and a great loss of life, before the German army surrendered Vimy Ridge to the Canadians.

"*The whole surface of the ground is a shapeless mess of broken trees, shell holes and ruined trenches. It is by far the worst sight I have ever seen, and the smells are sickening.*"

Leslie H. Miller

The white areas on Vimy Ridge look like snow — however, they are chalk. Soldiers tunnelled through the chalk, and while waiting for the battle to begin, some Canadian troops carved their names, hometowns, even faces into the tunnel walls. One hundred years later the carvings remain.

On the cold morning of April 9, 1917, Canadian artillery soldiers were photographed during the Battle of Vimy Ridge.

A German soldier stands amid ruined trees located within the territory of the commune of Givenchy-en-Gohelle, near where the Canadian National Vimy Memorial stands today.

"The next day," wrote Leslie, "I was out over the top [on the battlefield] carrying wounded and I was up as far as Thélus village. It is utterly destroyed by our shellfire." A few days later, Leslie climbed the ruined towers of the abbey at Mont-Saint-Éloi to look down upon "the splendid view of all Vimy Ridge, Arras and the high ground south and east of that town." While on the ridge, Leslie had gathered acorns from blasted oak trees.

Leslie mailed the acorns, tiny bundles of life, to his family in Canada. He could not have imagined then what would result one hundred years later from his pocketful of promise.

Sadly, the capture of Vimy Ridge, a battle credited with bringing world respect and acknowledgement to Canada, did not mark the end of war. There would still be more than another year of conflict.

On November 11, 1918, at eleven o'clock in the morning, the armistice was signed and the war stopped. Leslie Miller was made an Education Officer for Signals, and as troops prepared to be sent back home, he continued to use wireless sets for army communications. Leslie didn't leave the battlefields until February 15, 1919. By spring, now-Lieutenant Leslie H. Miller was back on the Millers' Ontario farm.

Returning soldiers made new plans for their futures. Leslie went back to university as a modern languages student but left when he contracted scarlet fever. He travelled back to Saskatchewan to teach but again had to change his plans. He returned to Ontario, and on the twenty-four acres of Miller farmland that was given to him, Leslie built a house, farmed, and nurtured the oak saplings that had sprouted from the acorns he gathered on Vimy Ridge.

In 1926, Leslie married Mary Isabel Fraser, "Essie," a teacher he had met before the war. Together they built up their farm and called it The Vimy Oaks. They never became parents but always welcomed visits from their nephews, and included young people in their life and work on the farm. Surrounded by orchards and productive fields, Leslie shared his war experiences of ruined lands and never-forgotten friends.

The two pips on Leslie's shoulder strap tell us he is a lieutenant. The cap and collar badges say "Canadian Engineers" and the rectangular "French Grey" patch on his upper arm says "3rd Canadian Division."

Leslie Miller's farm, The Vimy Oaks, in the 1920s. In the decades to come, beehives, a greenhouse and larger garden plots were added to the farm.

During the 1920s, while Leslie and Essie Miller were building a new life, nations mourned the millions who had died in the war and began to build monuments to honour them. Military cemeteries were designed to give the fallen soldiers permanent graves that their families might later visit.

In 1920, the Canadian Battlefields Memorials Commission held a design competition for memorials in France and Belgium. One hundred and sixty drawings were sent to the commission by Canadian artists; seventeen were selected as finalists. The winner, Toronto sculptor and monument designer Walter Seymour Allward, told how his design came to him:

"I dreamed that I was in a great battlefield. I saw our men going by in thousands and being mowed down . . . I turned my eyes and found myself looking down on an avenue of poplars. Suddenly through the avenue I saw thousands marching to the aid of our armies. They were the dead [who] entered the fight to aid the living. . . . Without the dead we were helpless . . . we owed them and will forever owe them."

Tourists, including disabled veterans of the First World War, began to visit the battlefields of the western front in the 1920s. Here, visitors view the Vimy trenches.

Allward's memorial was to be built on Hill 145, the highest point of Vimy Ridge, overlooking the Douai Plain on land granted to Canada by France in 1922 in recognition of Canada's war contributions. Work on the monument began three years later. A gigantic concrete and steel base was built with care — wartime tunnels and unexploded shells were just below the work crews. Where the vast Canadian Expeditionary Force had been part of a crucial victory in 1917, a symbol of the great loss of life and need for peace and everlasting remembrance was rising.

Walter S. Allward stands beside the winning maquette (model) he entered in the war memorial competition.

The statues on the Vimy monument were made by stone carvers who worked outdoors on-site. Here, the carvers work on the group of figures called *The Defenders: The Breaking of the Sword.*

21

First World War airplanes flew over a crowd of more than 100,000 on the day the Canadian National Vimy Memorial in France was dedicated. The statue of Mother Canada (also called Canada Bereft) was carved by Italian sculptor Luigi Rigamonti. Still draped with a British flag, she awaits her unveiling by King Edward VIII.

Thousands of Canadians sailed to France for the unveiling of the monument at Vimy on July 26, 1936. Some of those who crowded around the memorial were veterans of the Battle of Vimy Ridge; others were the parents or wives of soldiers who hadn't survived the war. As King Edward VIII of the United Kingdom removed the flag draping the figure of Mother Canada, he spoke of how "already the scars of war have well-nigh vanished from the fair landscape spread before us. Around us here today there is peace and rebuilding of hope."

Trees were again flourishing above the wartime tunnels; farms were green and harvests were sustaining life once more. Pines grew to whisper in the winds near the empty trenches; maples lined the road. But there were no longer any oak trees on Vimy Ridge.

Leslie never went back to France after the war. He and Essie farmed. A second war (1939–1945) engulfed the world; many of the sons and daughters of those who fought in the First World War served overseas. After the fighting ceased, people from around the globe had to rebuild their lives; some moved to other lands.

Many immigrants to Canada settled near Toronto during the 1950s and 1960s. Leslie, in his seventies by then, needed more help with his farm and orchard. He invited some of the new families to plant gardens on his land. His ability to speak many languages meant he could communicate with them. In exchange for the produce they grew, the immigrant families helped "Mr. Miller" harvest apples. The plots grown by the families at The Vimy Oaks were some of the first community gardens in the Toronto area.

Monty McDonald, the boy who had turned into the Miller driveway with his family in 1951, often helped out on the farm, as did the two Miller nephews and other local boys. They harnessed and drove Leslie's team of horses to pull loads of produce or brush. There was also time for diving into piles of hay in the barn.

Sometimes, Leslie suddenly called out for work to stop. "Listen," he'd tell the puzzled boys. "It's the grasshopper sparrow, a rare bird." Like many soldiers, Leslie suffered from hearing loss after the war, but that didn't keep him from listening for the high-pitched calls of the birds that lived in the many trees on the Miller farm.

As teenagers, the boys helped Leslie with heavier work on the farm, scything, digging, removing dead fruit trees and helping with the apple harvest. With Leslie as their employer and teacher, they learned how to identify plants and wildlife, to name the constellations and how to work in harmony with nature.

Leslie and his wife, Essie, sold their farm in 1965 and moved into an apartment just a few kilometres away from The Vimy Oaks. Always a teacher, Leslie continued to share information about nature with the schoolchildren who walked with their teachers through a nearby park. His interest in all aspects of the natural world continued until his death in 1979, at age ninety. Essie died in 1984. The boys who had worked on the farm were adults with their own families and memories of the Vimy Oaks — both the farm and the trees.

Some of the Vimy oaks growing at the edge of the Miller farm were removed when the nearby road was widened. Over decades, industrial buildings replaced the farmhouse and orchards. By 2007, a local church congregation had bought the property and built their new place of worship on it. The remains of the Miller woodlot can be seen from the church's chapel.

Daniel, one of Leslie and Essie's nephews, enjoyed a ride on Rose during a family visit to The Vimy Oaks in 1957.

Essie, and Leslie with a feline friend, 1955.

The oaks that remained grew taller and wider. Passersby didn't know they were shaded by more than lush green leaves; they were in the presence of history.

"I am writing seated at the foot of a large oak," Leslie Miller wrote in 1916, while war raged around him. Little could he have imagined how many generations of families would enjoy the oaks he nurtured in Canada.

In 2004, Monty McDonald took a long-awaited trip to France, to follow the routes his father had taken during the Second World War. Monty also visited First World War battlefields in France and Belgium. A stop along Vimy Ridge was a priority. Monty walked around the imposing Canadian National Vimy Memorial and along the *Chemin des Canadiens*. He could only imagine what Leslie Miller had seen there nearly one hundred years earlier.

Beyond the ridge were villages, like Thélus and Givenchy-en-Gohelle, that Leslie had seen in ruins in 1917 but had since been rebuilt. What Monty did *not* see were oak trees. Leslie Miller's oaks from Vimy were still growing — but an ocean away. "What if?" Monty thought. What if Vimy Ridge could be green again, with oak trees descended from Leslie's Ontario trees?

Mature maple trees line the road that passes by the Canadian National Vimy Memorial.

The landscape near the memorial still undulates with the craters made by explosions during the battle. Pine trees shadow the trenches and sheep graze nearby. The grass covers still-dangerous explosives that have been buried for one hundred years.

Oak trees are symbols of strength and endurance. The *Quercus robur* (Latin name for the English/French oak) is the "Vimy Oak" grown by Leslie Miller in Canada.

Like the expression "Mighty oaks from little acorns grow," the idea sprouted. Tree experts confirmed that the oak trees in the Miller woodlot were *not* trees native to Canada. They were English/French oaks, the kind that once grew on Vimy Ridge. The kind that Lieutenant Leslie H. Miller had seen destroyed by war. An exciting adventure was about to begin . . .

Interest in the repatriation of oak trees, descendants of Leslie Miller's specimens, grew quickly. The Vimy Oaks Repatriation Project was covered by the Canadian media; people worked towards ensuring that Miller oaks would grow once more on Vimy Ridge and at selected places of remembrance in Canada.

On a frosty day in January 2015, arborists from a garden nursery climbed the Miller oaks and removed scions — the most recent growth — from the tops of the trees while they were dormant. The scions were grafted on to English oak saplings from British Columbia.

As the oaks grew, they were moved from a warm greenhouse to a larger building where the temperatures were more typical of outdoor conditions. Small pots were exchanged for larger ones as the trees flourished. In the spring of 2016, the young trees were moved outdoors to thrive in typical conditions. During the summer, more saplings, this time grown from acorns harvested from the Miller oaks, joined them. Hundreds of "Vimy Oaks," symbols of remembrance, would be ready soon to be planted across Canada.

Professional arborist Andrew Cowell climbs high into one of the Miller oaks to collect cuttings called scions.

"The roads are lined with poplars, continuous rows rising to near 60 feet in height and spreading their crowns to meet inward and form an arch. We were marching through an avenue arched over with foliage far overhead and carpeted below with the forest's few leaves of autumn's gathering."
Leslie H. Miller

Oak trees produced by either grafting or planted acorns resulted in sturdy "soldiers" lined up in an Ontario nursery and reaching the ceiling of the growing area.

Acorns are the fruit of an oak tree. Inside each acorn there is usually one seed. The "cap" of the acorn is called a cupule. Some acorns are small and round; the Vimy Oaks' acorns are oval.

Meanwhile in France, other trees were being grown from acorns gathered beneath the shady branches of Leslie Miller's soaring oaks in Canada. On November 11, 2018, the one-hundredth anniversary of the end of the First World War, these saplings will be growing along Vimy Ridge and in the Vimy Foundation Centennial Park near the Canadian National Vimy Memorial.

Symbols of peace, justice and remembrance are incorporated into the Canadian National Vimy Memorial. Just as the two white pylons of the monument reach to the sky, the new oaks will tower over future generations of visitors. They will call upon us to remember the past — and a Canadian soldier who once held hope and rebirth in the palm of his hand.

"When walking through this promenade [of trees], we found it so calm while a strong wind was blowing outside, the light so strangely softened and diffused, and the gentle rustling of the leaves so soothing a sound that the place seemed like a bit of fairyland."
Leslie H. Miller

Glossary

Arborist — a specialist in the planting, care and maintenance of trees

Armistice — the official end of a war

Douai Plain — the open area below Vimy Ridge

First World War — also called the Great War, the War to End All Wars and
    World War I, 1914–1918

Leave — a soldier's official, permitted time away from the battlefield

Repatriation — return to the country of origin

Scarlet fever — a contagious disease with high fever and a red (scarlet) skin
    eruption

Scion — a detached woody shoot containing buds, used in grafting

Trench fever — a highly contagious disease transmitted by body lice to soldiers;
    they suffered from weakness, fever, a rash and leg pains

Wireless set — equipment used to communicate by sending signals through
    the air

"Shell Hole Swim" is how Leslie Miller described this 1917 snapshot of the bath
he took in a water-filled shell hole near Souchez, France. Soldiers kept their
protective steel helmets on even when bathing. Just in case . . .

Index

Acknowledgements

I am grateful that I did not travel alone across the massive battlefields of the past and beneath the towering trees of the present. Heartfelt thanks are extended to the talented crew at Scholastic Canada Ltd.: Sandy Bogart Johnston, who shared with me a first visit to Leslie Miller's Vimy Oaks; Diane Kerner, an ever-supportive publisher; Anne Shone, who gallantly picked up the torch as this project grew; Aldo Fierro, who designed pages that sing; and Brian Deines, illustrator *extraordinaire*.

Gratitude also goes to those who variously offered their time and expertise: Patricia Sinclair, Vimy Oaks Project Coordinator; Brandt Miller and Daniel Miller, nephews of Leslie H. Miller; Richard (Kathy) Breakey, great-nephew of Leslie H. Miller; Lynda Kuehn, great-niece of Leslie H. Miller; the Scarborough Chinese Baptist Church, Scarborough, Ontario; Melissa Mikel, remembrance educator; Dorothy Proudler; Monty McDonald, President, the Vimy Oaks Legacy Corporation, and the late Stitch; Caitlin Ayling, Case Vanderkruk and Andrew Barbour, NVK Holdings Inc., Waterdown, Ontario; Jeremy Diamond and Jennifer Blake, the Vimy Foundation; Tim Cook and Arlene Doucette, Canadian War Museum; the "Givenchy 2017/année du Canada" committee of Givenchy-en-Gohelle, France; Diane Turbide; Robert Symons; Mary Hocaliuk, Archives of Manitoba; the staff of Library and Archives Canada; Alexandre Bellemare, Veterans Affairs Canada.

Finally, as ever, many thanks and much love to Cal Smiley, Devon Smiley, Brian Smiley, Felicia Torchia and Cyrus Joseph Smiley, who, like this book, is a 2017 "new arrival."

Credits

Grateful acknowledgement is made to all those who have granted permission to reprint copyrighted and personal material. Every reasonable effort has been made to locate the copyright holders for these images. The author and publisher would be pleased to receive information that would allow them to rectify any omissions in future printings.

Archival photographs are courtesy of members of the Miller Family, except where noted. Items from The Granfield Collection are noted as TGC.

Page 2: courtesy of Dorothy Proudler; 8: (upper) TGC, (lower) Archives of Manitoba, L. B. Foote fonds, Foote 2303. Parade on Portage Ave. [c1915], N2965; (lower) TGC; 11: (upper right) TGC; (lower) by Montague B. Black; 12: (upper) TGC; 16: TGC; 20: TGC; 21: Courtesy of Veterans Affairs Canada; 22: TGC; 28: TGC; 30: Courtesy of Robert Symons; 31: TGC